ALCATRAZ

THE OFFICIAL GUIDE

by Paul McHugh

GOLDEN GATE NATIONAL PARKS CONSERVANCY
SAN FRANCISCO, CALIFORNIA

SOLDIER OVERLOOKING MAIN ROAD
TO THE TOP OF THE ISLAND, C. 1900

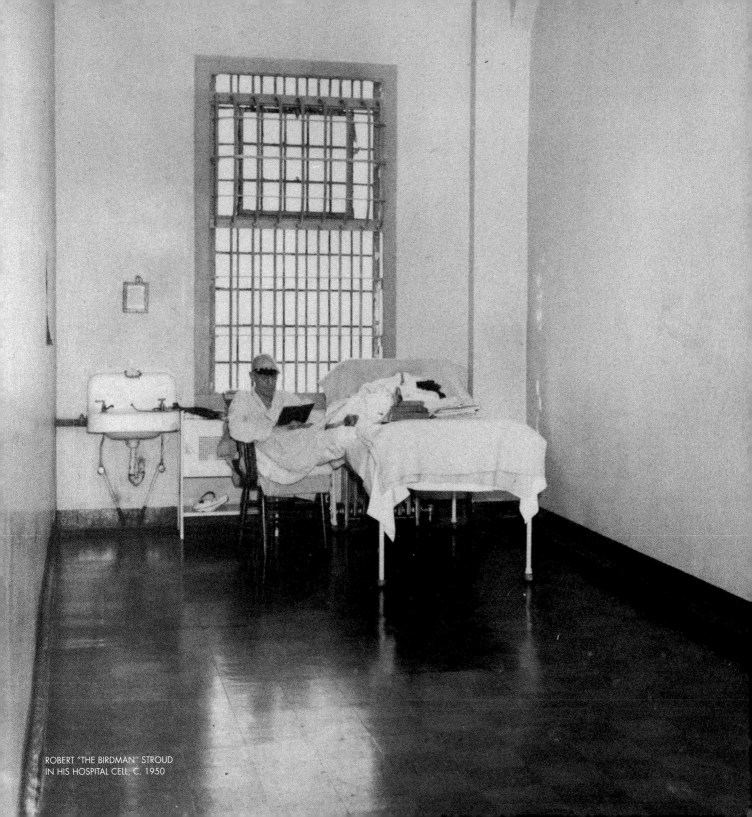

ROBERT "THE BIRDMAN" STROUD
IN HIS HOSPITAL CELL, C. 1950

INSIDE THE ROCK

Alcatraz is a natural sentinel, a small, domed island jutting up just three miles inside San Francisco Bay amid the broad sea lanes that lead in from the Pacific Ocean through the Golden Gate strait. The sweeping, grand vistas of bridge, ocean, and city—visible, at least, when the fog is out—offer dramatic contrasts to the narrow horizons defined by prison cells and perimeter fences. A maze of brick and concrete walls broken by narrow doors leads visitors deep into the island's history as a federal and military prison and Civil War fortress.

Confinement, or the threat of it, controlled those who resisted US policy, including American Indians and recalcitrant soldiers. Similarly, wiseguys, miscreants, and murderers saw tempered steel bars slam shut when they shredded legal and civil norms during the Depression and Prohibition times, and they heard the pop of rifle shots and boom of gas grenades if those bars were spread even slightly. The island's resident birds—some of whom are busily taking great advantage of its unnatural human modifications—provide us with a door into its natural world.

Among the literal Alcatraz passageways that can be seen today are the big arched door of the dockside sally port, where artillerymen and riflemen were prepared to repel any of the Confederacy's "Johnny Rebs"; the door of a tiny morgue, where bodies were taken before being transported to the mainland; and a door in the floor, opening to a stairwell leading down from a walkway west of D Block. Down through that shadowy hole, especially obstreperous convicts could be dragged, screaming and cursing, into a damp, echoing "dungeon" cell—once a coal bin in the moat of the Civil War-era Citadel—then shackled to doors or ringbolts. (These subterranean cells were used for solitary confinement until D Block's "modern" isolation cells were completed.)

MODERN-DAY VIEWS—WESTERN GULLS; LOOKING EAST TOWARD THE BAY BRIDGE; REMNANTS OF PRISON-ERA GARDEN SHED; INMATE HOSPITAL CELL

Upstairs, at the north end of C Block, is a special sheet-steel door leading to the recreation yard. It was locked in 1946 when Coy, Cretzer, Hubbard, Thompson, Carnes, and Shockley tried to escape. Because they couldn't find key #107, which opened this door, they were trapped in the cellhouse, and three of them (Coy, Cretzer, and Hubbard) eventually died after being hit by bullets and shrapnel during what became known as "the Battle of Alcatraz." Miran Thompson, Sam Shockley, and Clarence Carnes were tried for the murder of a guard; Thompson and Shockley were executed at San Quentin for their part in the escape attempt, while Carnes—spared because of his youth—was returned to prison.

Prison history and artifacts are doors into fantasies of confinement, doors that can be easily exited into the fresh air and independent movement of which inmates could only dream. We are particularly drawn to the dark romance of the federal prison era on Alcatraz Island, mesmerized, perhaps, by decades of Hollywood's celluloid fantasies highlighting the bars, barbed wire, and barbarities of "the Rock."

Yet, this speck of land in San Francisco Bay—shaped like a battleship plowing through the bay's rush of cold tidal currents just inside the Golden Gate strait—boasts many more layers of significance. In fact, it's so packed with experiences of various types that when it comes to surprises per square yard, Alcatraz may well offer more to a visitor than any other place in the Golden Gate National Recreation Area (GGNRA), the grand, 80,000-acre Bay Area National Park Service unit to which the rocky isle belongs. Foot for foot, this 22-acre island may even provide more than any other park in the system.

As one stepped through the [recreation wall] gate, the view was beautiful. Directly in front was the Golden Gate Bridge and to the left was San Francisco. Each day, this was a reminder of the freedom, love, and good things in life we had lost by our crimes.

— Jim Quillen, Alcatraz Inmate #586, *Alcatraz from Inside*

Cell doors slide into position with a final metal-to-metal collision that echoes throughout the concrete building.

— Jolene Babyak, *Eyewitness on Alcatraz*

"I never grow tired of this place," says the GGNRA's chief of public affairs, Rich Weideman, during a visit. "Started as a seasonal ranger here in 1981, and I just fell in love with Alcatraz. Everything you see out here is a cultural landscape." As Weideman notes, on Alcatraz, even natural values are artificial, a result of human activity. For example, centuries ago, before Europeans arrived, Alcatraz was a white-streaked sandstone hump (which likely supported little more than some native grasses and chaparral plants) in the bay, and a major seabird rookery and roosting spot. Once the island began to be used for military and prison purposes, most of the birds sought more congenial—not to mention quieter—sites. Now, Alcatraz is regaining its bird-friendly status. These birds are not returning to the same intact landscape their distant ancestors colonized, however, but to one altered by human activities. And they've been successful in exploiting this new environment. Black-crowned night herons use rubble from demolished buildings and thickets of non-native plants as new nesting areas. Western gulls make use of patches of concrete.

Brandt's cormorants perch on cliff ledges, some of which have been created or altered by pickaxe and dynamite.

Even these landscapes are layered. Those drawn to the big prison building may be forgiven for thinking it old. However, that huge, early–20th-century concrete cube sits atop what remains of even earlier Civil War-era defensive barracks built of brick (a fact that has demanded significant and expensive modern-day engineering and retrofitting to ensure the safety of this whole ensemble). It takes time to grasp everything this tiny island holds. That's one of the things that makes probing its mysteries so intriguing.

Follow one thread through what Alcatraz has to offer, and you trace the history of the American Indian civil rights movement. Follow another, and you get a picture of the challenges modern wildlife face, as well as the swift gains nature can make when humans work in partnership instead of opposition. Crime and punishment? That story is writ quite large here, an epic with many chapters.

Every time visitors walk through the ferry gate on the San Francisco waterfront to take the short ride across the bay to Alcatraz, their fares help fund and facilitate the reconstruction and stabilization of the island they are heading out to see.

By the simple act of looking, visitors help make sure that there are things to look at. Have fun exploring—it's your well-spent nickel.

MODERN-DAY DOORWAY; WARDEN'S RESIDENCE, C. 1934; LIGHTHOUSE BEAM; GULL EGGS; VIEW FROM ALCATRAZ, C. 1890

THE NATURE OF ALCATRAZ
GEOLOGY

When people say, "It's just the tip of an iceberg," they're talking about the visible part of a mass of polar ice, four-fifths of which is below water.

Similarly, when you stand on the crest of Alcatraz, you are actually standing on the tip of an almost-drowned mountain. Fifteen thousand years ago, a sandstone stack would have spread out beneath your feet. Around its base, you would have seen the floor of what is today San Francisco Bay, a broad, rumpled valley with forests of cedar and pine interspersed with broad reaches of dunes through which numerous rivers flowed.

But one thing you wouldn't have seen is the Pacific Ocean. Back then, the seashore lay 32 miles west, 6 miles past the cluster of tall rocks we now call the Farallon Islands. Out there, at the edge of the Continental Shelf, the mighty Sacramento River finally met the sea.

The Continental Shelf is the leading edge of a giant, geologic mass of granite and basalt known as the North American Plate. Sixty to 180 million years ago, as the Earth's plates ground past and over each other, the North American Plate scraped up old sediment layers, volcanic extrusions, and ancient hunks of vanished landforms, which gradually merged, folded, faulted, and uplifted. Taken as a whole, they formed a jumble of rock groups (terranes) called the Franciscan Complex. The island we know as Alcatraz is the namesake of the Alcatraz terrane, the oldest layer, made primarily of thick graywacke sandstone containing quartz and feldspar, as well as a small amount of chert.

This Island is chiefly composed of irregularly stratified sandstone covered with a thin coating of guano. The stone is full of seams in all directions which render it unfit for any building purposes & probably difficult to quarry. The island has no beach & but two or three points where small boats can land.

— Lt. William Warner, US Topographical Engineers, 1847

Through the millennia, as ice sheets melted and sea waters rose, this mountain became an island, a bare little hump protruding above the waters of the bay. Separated from terrestrial predators by the rising waters, birds on Alcatraz had a safe nesting haven, and they utilized it in great numbers.

Today, with access limited by both safety concerns and bird nesting requirements, it's not easy to see evidence of the island's geologic past. It can be observed, however, in the cuts along the switchback path to the top of the island. At the first switchback, look for a layer about a foot thick dipping steeply to the east. According to Ted Konigsmark in *Geologic Trips: San Francisco and the Bay Area*, the sandstone here is "light yellow-brown in color and feels like sandpaper" when rubbed (details below). And along the West Road below the prison, look up at the massive cliff underlying the recreation yard, another dramatic example of the island's geologic record.

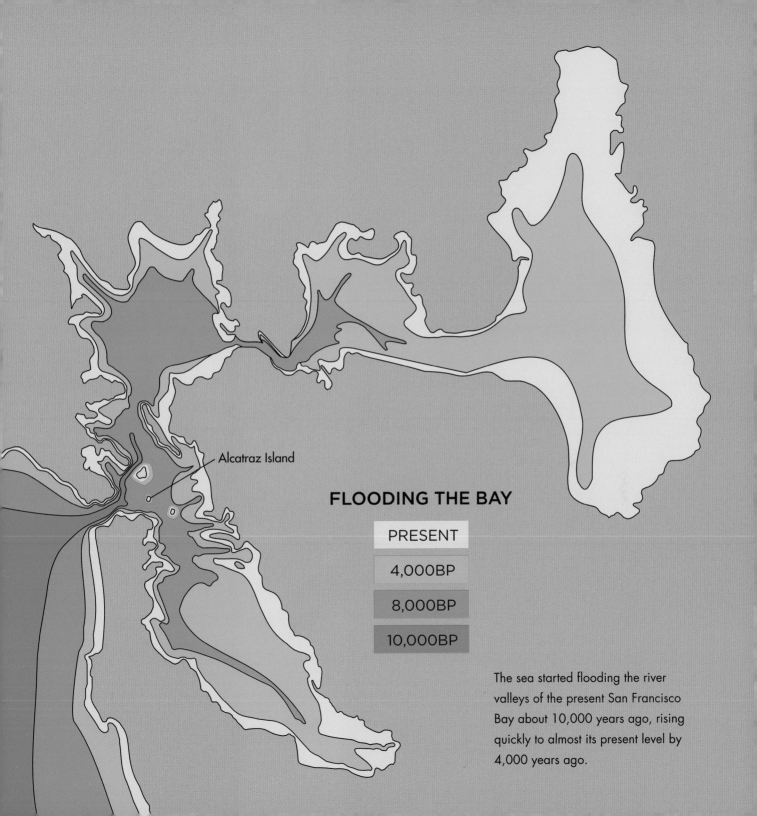

Alcatraz Island

FLOODING THE BAY

PRESENT

4,000BP

8,000BP

10,000BP

The sea started flooding the river valleys of the present San Francisco Bay about 10,000 years ago, rising quickly to almost its present level by 4,000 years ago.

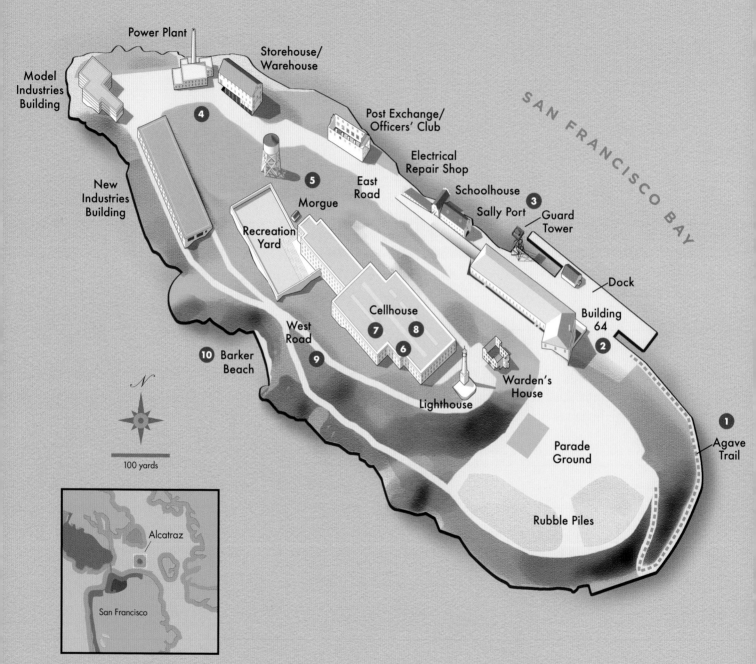

ALCATRAZ ISLAND

Power Plant

Storehouse/ Warehouse

Model Industries Building

Post Exchange/ Officers' Club

Electrical Repair Shop

New Industries Building

East Road

Schoolhouse

Sally Port

Guard Tower

Morgue

Recreation Yard

Dock

Building 64

West Road

Cellhouse

Barker Beach

Warden's House

Lighthouse

N

100 yards

Parade Ground

Agave Trail

Rubble Piles

SAN FRANCISCO BAY

Alcatraz

San Francisco

FOLLOW THE RANGER
ISLAND TOUR

To help you explore Alcatraz, you're invited to track down the following. Think of this as a cultural treasure hunt.

1. Agave Trail
This route, framed by its namesake plant, which helps stabilize the soil on the island's southern slope, is a relic of the military era. Because birds nest nearby during the spring and summer months, it is only open September through January.

2. Bombproof Barracks (Building 64), Dock Area
This building is also a military relic. As you walk through the lower floor, look at the sturdy brick arches that mark the casemated barracks where 19th-century artillerymen slept, ready to spring into action. During the federal prison period, the area was used as a guards' locker room, WWII air raid shelter, and general storehouse.

3. Sally Port Cannon
Look to your left as you pass through the arched gate on your hike up the Main Road. A cannon set in a wide embrasure is positioned to blast any force trying to test the moat and gate, a blend of medieval and modern defensive systems.

4. Military Tunnel
Join one of the walking tours to see more than you can strolling on your own. A normally closed gate on the East Road leads past the old Quartermaster Building to a long tunnel hacked through rock at the north end of the island, built in the 1870s to allow concealed passage of soldiers and supplies.

5. Prison Morgue
At a switchback in the main road, near the north end of the prison, is a small structure with an open steel door, a grated skylight, and a dank and mossy examination table. Despite its spooky ambiance, this morgue had only one documented use, overnight storage of the body of a prisoner who died after the last boat run.

6. Cellhouse Visitor Windows
Just inside the main cellhouse entrance, look to your left to see a row of thick windows, each flanked by steel panels rather like horse blinders. Although these were designed to allow visitors to communicate, they actually reinforced the prisoners' isolation. Inmates could have one visit per month from an immediate family member or another approved guest.

7. Cellhouse Battle Scars
On the cutoff corridor for C Block, which connects "Broadway" with the library area, look down to see shrapnel scars in the concrete, and up to see a hole chopped in the roof. That's where US Marines lowered grenades tied to cords during the 1946 "Battle of Alcatraz."

8. Dungeon Stairs
The aisle on the east side of A Block is typically locked, but can be opened for ranger or volunteer-led tours. A low, U-shaped wall marks the top of a flight of stairs leading down to the old Citadel basement under the cellhouse, where recalcitrant prisoners were sequestered during the prison's early years.

9. Garden Shed
Outside, on the West Road, look for a crumbling, glassed-in shed underneath a tree. This is where inmate gardeners nurtured blooms for planting in the terraced gardens.

10. Barker Beach
Farther along, where the West Road doubles back to the south, walk straight to the railing and look over the cliff at a small, pebbled beach in the cove. This was where Arthur "Doc" Barker, son of the infamous Ma Barker, was shot and killed during an escape attempt in 1939.

ALCATRAZ ISLAND, 1890

CIVIL WAR-ERA CANNON AND OFFICERS; WAITING FOR THE LAUNCH; BRAND-NEW PRISON BUILDING, 1912; MILITARY INMATES, NOON COUNT, C. 1905

FORTRESS ALCATRAZ
1854 – 1933

Loose lips don't always sink ships. Sometimes, they save them.

That's what occurred in San Francisco Bay during the Civil War, when a newly fortified Alcatraz Island played a role in helping authorities thwart the only attempted blockade of the bay by a Confederate privateer. That it was a spy ship only makes the story that much more intriguing.

Unfortunately for the success of its mission, the schooner *JM Chapman* had a newly hired captain who happened to be a blabbermouth when he drank. In the grogshops, fleshpots, and bordellos of San Francisco's rollicking Barbary Coast waterfront, Captain William C. Law let it slip that he—a formerly respectable employee of the Pacific Mail Steamship Co.— had been hired for a project that could shift the course of the entire war. Yes, three prominent "Copperheads," local Southern sympathizers, were involved. Yes, they might belong to Knights of the Golden Circle, a secret society. He could say no more...

Whatever Law actually said, he had already said too much. At sunrise on March 15, 1863, the *Chapman* set sail and drifted languidly away from the San Francisco wharves. A vessel of 90 tons, she supposedly carried mining supplies for Mexico, but was actually laden with cannon, munitions, uniforms, and provisions for Confederate privateers. The score of rebels aboard aimed to use Law's expertise to commandeer a mail steamer, then participate in blockading the bay, seizing its forts, and capturing the vast stream of gold and silver bullion that flowed from California's mines and Nevada's Comstock Lode, revenue that could finance the Confederacy's war effort. At minimum, just depriving the North of all that money would greatly assist the South.

But the USS *Cyane*, a sloop-of-war with twenty-two cannon and two hundred sailors, a ship of the tiny United States Pacific Squadron, already lay in wait for the rebel schooner. So did the steam tug *Anashe*, with its heavily armed complement of San Francisco police officers and customs police.

After all, *Chapman* had lied on her manifest.

Two ship's boats from the *Cyane* reached her first. The *Anashe* had been delayed; its crew was watching Captain Law, who stood on the pier, waving and hollering for the *Chapman* to return. After a night hitting the sauce, Law was so late to his rendezvous that the co-conspirators had decided to set sail without him. (Too bad they hadn't decided upon that exact maneuver six months earlier.)

The federals searched the schooner and found armaments, as well as a dozen or more rebels armed with revolvers and bowie knives playing hide-and-seek behind an impromptu hatch sawn into a bulkhead. All were taken under tow by the tug *Anashe* to the military prison on Alcatraz.

John C. Fremont (photo above) had seen Alcatraz's potential years earlier. Famed as "The Pathfinder," Fremont mounted no less than seven mapping and surveying expeditions of the American West, covering some 20,000 miles. Conveniently, Brevet Captain Fremont was on his third trip west when the Bear Flag Revolt broke out in California in 1846. His talent for keeping one eye on the main chance was helped immeasurably by his marriage to Jessie Benton, daughter of Senator Thomas Hart Benton, a champion of Manifest Destiny, a doctrine declaring that the United States was intended by providence to control North America from coast to coast.

Fremont added his scouting force of sixty-two men to several dozen buckskin-clad fur trappers and frontiersmen. Their presence and the pressure of the US Navy—as well as the willingness of *Californios* (citizens of Mexico living in Alta, or upper, California) to depart from the mother country's control—brought California into the Union in 1848 as a possession, ceded to the US by Mexico just weeks after gold was discovered at Sutter's Mill on the American River and before the implications of the discovery were known.

Fremont's military training and topographic experience led him to select Alcatraz as key to

---

1775 Captain Juan Manuel de Ayala sails the *San Carlos* into San Francisco Bay, the first penetration by a European vessel. He explores the bay and charts Alcatraz and the other principal islands

AT LEFT: CITADEL WITH CANNONBALL ORNAMENTATION, C. 1890

1846 The Mexican governor of Alta California grants the island of Alcatraz to an Anglo *Californio* from Los Angeles, who transfers title to his son-in-law. Then, in June of that year, the Bear Flag rebellion upsets the *Californio* applecart.

1847 Army engineers survey Alcatraz, with a view toward retaining the most strategic properties for use by the Union.

1848 Mexico cedes California to the US and gold is discovered at Sutter's Mill on the American River.

WALKING UP THE MAIN ROAD, C. 1920; ORIGINAL LIGHTHOUSE, C. 1900; SPANISH-AMERICAN WAR SOLDIER; ALCATRAZ FROM BLACK POINT, C. 1865

> The sandstone composing the Island is very friable; even where hardened on the surface, it can be cut with a hatchet. Wrought iron spikes can be driven into the rock without much trouble.
>
> — Lt. Zealous B. Tower, 1853

commanding the entrance to the bay with artillery. Seeing it as "the best position for Lighthouse and Fortifications," he wangled a purchase contract for the island from the Californio who held the land-grant title. The army agreed with Fremont's evaluation, but did not recognize his claim, dismissing it entirely when Fremont was court-martialed for exceeding his command, as well as for general arrogance and disobedience.

Then, the military promptly took steps to realize Fremont's vision. Miners—known as the '49ers—poured through San Francisco on their way to the gold fields of the Sierra Nevada, and California became a state in 1850, at which point President Millard Fillmore reserved certain of its lands for government use. Construction of the West Coast's very first lighthouse began on Alcatraz in 1853, and light shone through its Fresnel lens the following year. Work also began on the island's fortifications, primarily, the Citadel—a three-story brick defensive barracks surrounded by a moat and accessed via drawbridges—on the crest of the island, and cannon emplacements around the island's perimeter.

By 1861, more than one hundred cannon were in place, mostly smoothbore Columbiads. There was also a "sally port," or gate, between the island's fortified crest and its docking area. In the earliest days, the sally port dungeon, or oubliette, was used to confine obstreperous soldiers, a place meant to take the starch out of them. You can still see the entrance hatch, though its lower walls have been knocked out.

"It would have been terrible to get thrown in that thing," says John Martini, a prominent Alcatraz

1849 The Gold Rush begins in earnest.

1850 California becomes a state and Alcatraz is reserved for military use.

1853 On Alcatraz, work begins on the West Coast's first lighthouse and perimeter fortification. In June of the following year, the lighthouse's beams can be seen 14 miles out to sea.

1856 Work begins on the Citadel.

1859 The first military prisoners are confined in a small dungeon under the sally port.

1861 The isolated island fortress becomes a military prison as well as an artillery post.

1876 A famous 4th of July demonstration of firepower from Bay Area forts fails to sink an anchored scow, demonstrating the defenses' shortcomings.

historian. "Just 11 feet wide and 19 feet long, with no privies. It must have seemed like the Black Hole of Calcutta."

When the Civil War exploded in 1861, more than 350 Union troops —primarily artillerymen— were stationed here. But the number of military police and guards began to increase as well, because that same year, Alcatraz was officially designated as the military prison for the Department of the Pacific. In 1862, the first wooden cellblock was built adjacent to the brick guardhouse.

Just in time to welcome miscreants from the *Chapman*. The lead Copperhead conspirators—Asbury Harpending, Ridgley Greathouse, and Alfred Rubery—answered to treason charges in an eight-day trial, and were found guilty after a mere four minutes of deliberation by the jury. They were assigned ten-year sentences. The remainder of the crew was released after taking an oath of allegiance to the Union. Following a presidential grant of freedom to political prisoners, the ringleaders had their sentences commuted the following year.

After the Civil War, the stream of prisoners consigned to Alcatraz continued to swell. Besides military-law-breaking soldiers, it included Hopis and Modocs from the West's Indian wars. Eventually, US soldiers convicted of crimes during the Philippine–American conflict, as well as WWI-era American conscientious objectors and deserters, were sampling the spartan accommodations and fresh sea air of Alcatraz.

Its early cellblocks bursting at their seams, the island was altered once more. The above-ground section of the Citadel was demolished in 1908, and the below-ground section was left to support a huge new prison building, which was completed in 1912. (That lower floor of the Civil War-era defensive barracks still exists in the darkness below the cellhouse.)

After two more decades of managing its expanded prison, in 1933, the military folded its flag for the last time and turned Alcatraz over to federal civilian authorities, who would operate the Rock as a maximum-security jail for "the worst of the worst" from 1934 to 1963.

1898 The Spanish–American war generates hundreds of military lawbreakers, and Alcatraz functions almost entirely as a prison.

1908 Construction of the modern-day, three-story concrete prison begins after the Citadel is dismantled down to its lower, below-ground level, which is retained as a basement for the prison building.

1909 The original 40-foot-tall lighthouse is torn down and replaced by an 84-foot-high concrete tower.

1912 Rumored to be the world's largest reinforced concrete building at the time, the new prison on Alcatraz is completed.

1915 Alcatraz is designated as a disciplinary barracks, focused on rehabilitation.

1933 The Department of Justice acquires title to Alcatraz from the military, and the Bureau of Prisons begins its transformation into a maximum-security civilian penitentiary.

AT RIGHT: ALCATRAZ DOCK AND THE STEAMER McPHERSON, 1869

TEN BEST PHOTO OPPORTUNITIES

Guard Tower

Standing on the docks, look north to see a recreation of a 60-foot-tall guard tower. Explore a variety of angles for the best shot.

Sally Port Garden

Some of the first Alcatraz gardens to be restored by the Garden Conservancy are in the strip alongside the road up to the sally port. Look for Victorian-era roses.

Warden's House

Up near the prison's entrance, look east to find the shell of the warden's house, which burned in 1970. Peer through the windows to get an angle on the ruined stonework of the mantle and fireplace. A beautiful, if melancholy shot. When the interior of the house fills with blooming red valerian, it seems somewhat more cheerful.

San Francisco Views

Walk around to the south side of the lighthouse for a variety of shots of San Francisco, and to the west (on clear days), of the Golden Gate Bridge.

Prison Entry

From the front of the warden's house, shoot an oblique wide-angle view of the prison.

Recreation Yard Door

Inside the cellhouse, go to the north end of C Block to see the stout steel door that opens to stairs leading down into the enclosed recreation yard. (This was the door the would-be escapees failed to open during the 1946 Battle of Alcatraz.) Frame a vertical shot capturing shadows at the edges of the door, looking down at the rec yard.

Wild Gardens

The most sumptuous and colorful turf on the island is found on the sloping ground in the corner between the rec yard and the prison building, on the west side. Try close-ups and wide angles on the blooms, and rack focus* on either the flowers in the foreground or the prison structures behind them.

Roosting Seabirds

At the overlook above Barker Beach, look either direction, to spot big black cormorants hanging out on the rocks, drying their wings and resting. During spring, two species nest here.

Nesting Shorebirds

Farther up the West Road, between the old potting shed and the lighthouse, look down to the southwest to spot nesting snowy egrets and black crowned night herons during spring and summer months.

Nesting Gulls

Look down on the parade ground in spring and summer to see the nests of Western gulls. During fall, when the gulls leave and the area is open to visitors, go to the south edge of the parade ground to shoot the Agave Trail.

*"Rack focus" is a technique in which a shot has two objects, one in the background, one in the foreground, one of which is in focus, one of which is not. To reverse the emphasis, adjust the camera lens. Racking the focus gives a variety of creative takes on the same subject.

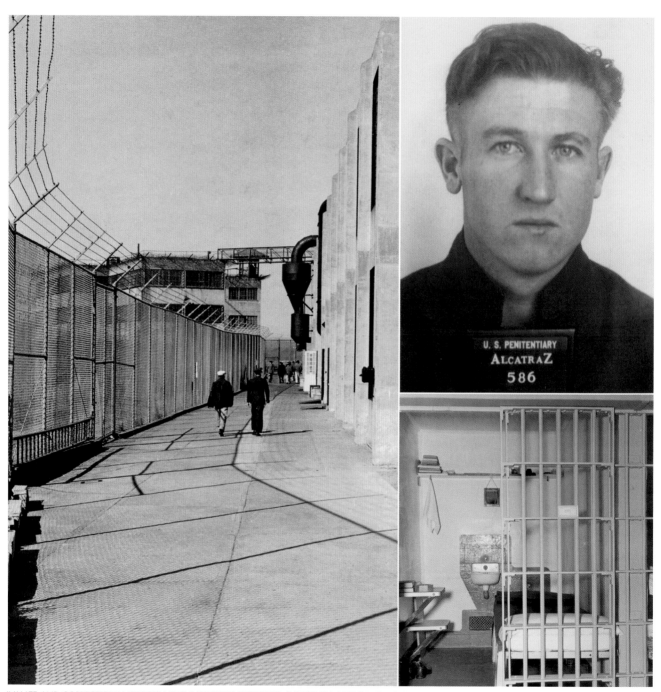

INMATE AND CORRECTIONAL OFFICER NEAR INDUSTRIES BUILDINGS; INMATE JIM QUILLEN, C. 1942; TYPICAL CELL

UNITED STATES PENITENTIARY ALCATRAZ ISLAND
1934 – 1963

Many Hollywood films have focused a lens on Alcatraz's federal prison era. Most of these movies were malarkey. A common theme was the torment of misunderstood prisoners by sadistic wardens.

No doubt about it, staffers at a maximum-security federal joint had to deploy tough measures to accomplish their jobs. But they did not ride herd on a collection of mildly soiled angels. Far from it. In the period 1934 to 1963, some of the most violent dregs of a criminal culture spawned by Prohibition and the Great Depression were consigned to the Rock.

Among the 1,576 men incarcerated here over a period of twenty-nine years (the prison held an average of 260 inmates at any one time), luminaries included George Kelly Barnes, AKA "Machine Gun" Kelly; Alvin "Creepy" Karpis; and "Scarface" Al Capone. Differences between a romantic view and a clear-eyed assessment of one "star" inmate—Robert Stroud, the so-called "Birdman of Alcatraz"— may help us grasp the gap between popular perception and the gruesome complexities of actual prison life.

Stroud, while indeed a self-taught bird expert, never got to be one on Alcatraz. His years of analyzing diseases in songbirds, publishing two books on the topic, and achieving some international renown came during a prior incarceration at Leavenworth (1912–1942). Within the system, he was far better known as a clever, manipulative nuisance. An anecdote from that period illustrates Stroud's talent for sly schemes. In 1936, FBI Director J. Edgar Hoover bought one of the famous Stroud's canaries as a present for his mother. But her little fowl, nicknamed "Jailbird," turned out to be a sparrow with its feathers dyed yellow.

Films have led us to believe that all prisoners continuously plot, conspire, and struggle to escape, and Stroud himself campaigned long and hard for parole. But when his big chance came to join an escape attempt during the "Battle of Alcatraz" in 1946, he not only declined that offer, he actively worked to minimize casualties and bring the episode to a close.

Even so, he was far from the sweet-tempered character portrayed by Burt Lancaster in the *Birdman* film of 1962. Stroud began his criminal career as an 18-year-old pimp for a 36-year-old hooker named Kitty O'Brien. He shot and killed a client of Kitty's who had beaten her after refusing to pay for her services. He shanked a fellow inmate at USP McNeil Island in Puget Sound (during his first stint at a federal B&B), and subsequently stabbed and killed a guard at Leavenworth.

Stroud's hobby of caring for sick birds and training them to perform tricks has been often been cited as a key to his character. But he had at least three more—and far less savory—prison pastimes: crafting concealable weapons, distilling alcohol from fruit mash, and penning rancid pornography. A film on the genuine Birdman would be more interesting but a lot harder to watch than the saccharine Lancaster opus.

Its climax would occur in May 1946, when six of Stroud's fellow prisoners overpowered guards and snatched their firearms and cellhouse keys. This is considered one of the island's most epic escape attempts. During the federal prison era, fourteen separate escapes were attempted by thirty-six individuals. Six escapees were shot and killed, twenty-three were nabbed, two were known to be drowned. The other five may have made it, but are likely to have drowned, their bodies washed out to sea. Of all these episodes, none had more drama than the Battle of Alcatraz.

It began when inmate librarian Bernie Coy and a cohort captured an unarmed guard (guards who had direct contact with inmates did not carry guns), trussed him up, stole his keys, and pitched him into a cell. Coy then removed his clothes, smeared grease on his body, and clambered, simian-like, up the bars more than twenty feet to the cellblock's west gun gallery. In his teeth, he held a bag containing contraband tools he used to spread the gallery bars enough to slip through. When a guard entered the gallery, Coy slammed a door into him, conked him with a riot club, then throttled the guard into unconsciousness with his own necktie.

1934 US Penitentiary Alcatraz opens; one of its early inmates, Alphonse Capone, arrives in August of that year for a four-year sojourn. James A. Johnston, its first warden, serves until 1948.

1938 The first guard dies on duty. Royal C. Cline is slain by a hammer blow during the third escape attempt. Guard Harold Stites shoots two of the three prisoners attempting to escape. (Stites himself would be shot and killed eight years later, in the Battle of Alcatraz.)

1946 Battle of Alcatraz follows thwarted escape attempt.

San Francisco Chronicle

ALCATRAZ SIEGE!
Photos of Prisoners' Rebellion!
One Guard Killed, 16 Injured

AT RIGHT: "BROADWAY," CORRIDOR BETWEEN CELLBLOCKS B AND C, C. 1934

> The public never wanted to know the real Alcatraz.... Even today after the prison has been closed for so many decades, the public just won't let go of the myths.
>
> — Phil Bergen, Captain of the Guards, USP Alcatraz

Next, Coy lowered the guard's keys and gun-gallery weapons to his co-conspirators: riot clubs, a Springfield 30.06 rifle with 50 rounds, and a Colt .45 pistol with three clips. More inmates were released, then nine other unarmed guards were over-powered and thrust into cells. Along with a frantic screech from the prison emergency sirens, a rumor shot from the island that the felons had armed themselves with machine guns. They hadn't. But authorities were sufficiently alarmed to summon the US Coast Guard and Marines. For two days, the cellblocks were wreathed in smoke and riddled with grenade shrapnel and flying bullets as an extremely uneven battle raged.

And at the height of the barrage Robert Stroud, then age 56, manifested a defining moment. He had already spent four years in a D-Block cell, the isolation tier. His was one of the doors opened by the escapees. Doors for other convicts had also been opened in hopes they would add to the general mayhem.

Instead, well aware that this rebellion would likely fail—especially since the rioters had not been able to locate a key that would let them exit the prison through the door to the rec yard, as they'd planned—many inmates cowered in their cells throughout the battle, under the thin protection of their mattresses.

One guard fighting to retake the cellhouse, Lt. Phil Bergen, watched in amazement as Stroud exited his cell on the third tier. As bullets whistled and rico-cheted, Stroud calmly dropped over the railing to the second tier, then down again to the main floor. Here, Stroud shoved shut the solid outer doors on the six solitary confinement cells to protect the convicts inside.

1962 Frank Morris and John and Clarence Anglin dig out of their cells and disappear in an elaborate, possibly successful escape plot (dramatized in a 1979 movie, *Escape from Alcatraz*, starring Clint Eastwood. Though many elements are fantasy, the portrayal is considered fairly accurate.) Later this year, two other prisoners bend bars in a kitchen window and try to swim to freedom. One is captured on a small rock near the island, the other, shivering and hypothermic, is nabbed on the mainland, near the southern terminus of the Golden Gate Bridge.

1963 Frustrated by the expense of running an island prison, and aware its concrete is crumbling (thus encouraging escape attempts), the Bureau of Prisons decides to shut down Alcatraz.

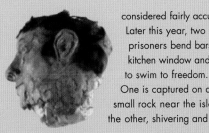

AT LEFT: AL CAPONE, ALCATRAZ INMATE #85; (PHOTO TAKEN 1929, FBI MUG SHOT)

INMATES IN RECREATION YARD; JAMES R. JOHNSTON, USP ALCATRAZ'S FIRST WARDEN; INMATES RETURNING TO CELLS FROM DINING HALL

Spotting Bergen, he shouted that no guns or rebels were in D Block. If authorities kept riddling it with gunfire, he said, blameless men would perish.

Then he casually clambered back up to his own cell by the same route.

In a book on Stroud by Jolene Babyak (daughter of the island's associate warden), Bergen is quoted as saying, "That person who is regarded as a monster by most people did the thing that none of the other, younger, inmates were willing to do. And he did it as easily as snapping your fingers."

After order was finally restored, this was the toll:

Two guards killed (one by friendly fire); three inmates killed, including Coy (two other conspirators would later be executed for their roles); seventeen guards and one inmate injured. There could easily have been at least one more casualty.

In her book, *Bird Man: The Many Faces of Robert Stroud*, Babyak says that the nasty-tempered, arrogant, manipulative Stroud had long been despised by both inmates and guards. After the battle subsided, she noted, most cells in D Block were marked by one or two bullet strikes. However, Stroud's cell, #41, displayed more than twenty pockmarks.

USP ALCATRAZ: AN INMATE'S DAY

7:00 AM A bell sounds, and you have 20 minutes to shave, dress, make your bed, and put your cell in order.

7:20 AM After a stand-up headcount (one of thirteen counts that occur in each 24-hour period), cell doors are racked open on each tier.

7:30 AM Breakfast in the mess hall. Eat as much as you want, and converse quietly. After 20 minutes, stack your utensils on your tray; guards account for every item. A guard with a Thompson submachine gun and a system that can automatically flood the mess hall with tear gas ensure peace and compliance.

7:50 AM If you're not assigned to a work detail, return to your cell. If you are, muster

in the rec yard, then head off to your shift. (During World War II, inmates laundered uniforms from Bay Area military bases and maintained submarine net buoys, which were retrieved and delivered to the island by the Navy for sandblasting, patching, and repainting.)

8:20–11:35 AM Work detail commences; you get one 10-minute smoke/rest break.

12:00 Noon After passing through a metal detector, you hit the mess hall again for lunch. After 20 minutes for chow, you are marched back to your cell for a half-hour break.

1:00–4:10 PM Leave your cell and go back to work; you get another 10-minute mid-period break in the afternoon.

4:40 PM Supper. Afterward, march back to your cell.

9:30 PM The day's last head count, and lights out.

BIRDS

Visitors are fascinated by the stories of hardened criminals and violent episodes from the island's military and federal prison eras, but the lives of the island's birds have always been far tougher.

For example, a pair of common ravens (*Corvus corax*), mated for life, have dominated on the Rock for more than a dozen years. "Those two ravens are the lions of the island," one ranger said. Like the huge tawny cats on the African veldt, these predators generally take what they want, when and how they want it. Big, tough, smart, and experienced, they boot their own offspring off the island after they fledge, and drive away raptors to maintain their preeminence.

Standing 2 feet tall, with a 4-foot wingspan (the male is slightly larger than the female), they fly as skillfully as any hawk. Highly intelligent, ravens work together to create a more successful hunt. When it's time to conduct predatory business, their thick, heavy bills, more than 3 inches long, can be as effective as steel chisels. Ravens, opportunistic feeders, are equally happy to kill small mammals such as mice or to poke holes in unattended plastic sandwich bags and gobble up the contents.

In early spring, when more than a thousand mated pairs of Western gulls construct their disorderly nests on almost any available flat spot and begin to lay eggs, not only do the ravens attack and devour eggs and young gull chicks, the gulls themselves (in defense of their individual territories) will kill the chicks of other gulls wandering too far from their home nests. Even humans find themselves a bit at risk. New naturalists and rangers—before they come to recognize the sound of diving gulls and learn to reflexively raise an arm to ward them off—are told to wear hard hats if they plan to enter the main gull nesting areas (which is discouraged altogether during nesting season) to protect from the random whack of a keen bill.

More than one hundred species of birds have been identified on Alcatraz; approximately eighteen species breed and nest here, and the rest drop by for seasonal roosting. However, one thing can unite them: Should a young hawk (most of the older ones know better!) cruise over Alcatraz, hunting for a quick lunch during nesting season, the whole island erupts in a screeching, swooping cacophony that lasts until the ignorant upstart is educated, and driven far away.

Usually, says biologist Chris Hellwig, the ravens spot the intruder and lead the charge, followed by a cloud of gulls. He once observed a juvenile red-shouldered hawk harried into the sea, where it drowned.

AT LEFT: RAVEN; THIS PAGE: WESTERN GULL AND CHICK; BROWN PELICAN; CORMORANTS.

Brandt's Cormorant

Big birds (nearly three feet tall), distinguished from other cormorants by black, scaly-looking feathers on their backs and yellow-colored throat pouches. They roost, feed, and nest on the island's perimeter.

Black-crowned Night Heron

Crepuscular hunters, the short, stocky night herons are most often seen standing guard above their nests on the island's upper west side, in the shadows under clumps of agave, ivy, and mirror plant.

Common Murre

This diving species, about half the size of a cormorant, doesn't nest on Alcatraz, but in spring or summer, may occasionally swim in from the Farallones, Pt. Reyes, and Devil's Slide with young in tow to forage.

Anna's Hummingbird

Bony old Alcatraz is the last place one would expect to spot the iridescent feathers of these tiny crimson-crowned birds, but ornamental gardens begun and maintained by soldiers, prisoners, and guards drew them in, and they continue to visit.

Canada Goose

These largest and most numerous of North America's geese have established a webbed foothold on Alcatraz, but they're having some difficulty making it a true honky-tonk. Less than a dozen mated pairs return annually, and they all have trouble keeping their chicks from being preyed upon by the gulls and ravens.

Black Oystercatcher

These sooty black birds resemble the sea-washed rocks they scramble across. A fancier of limpets, mussels, and sea worms, oystercatchers may also have been encouraged to come to Alcatraz by another manmade environment: tidepools created by construction debris. Only a few oystercatchers have been seen so far, but their strength of spirit bodes well.

Western Grebe

Grebes come to the Bay Area and other Pacific Coast sites to mate, a ritual that resembles a footrace, with the participants paddling and flapping across the water so rapidly it looks as though they're running across its surface. These birds are commonly seen in large numbers near the island during the winter and early spring months.

Brown Pelican

Though under the Endangered Species Act, brown pelicans have enjoyed a bit of a renaissance, they are still listed as federally endangered in California and much of the remainder of the country (they are also on the state's endangered-species list). Folding their wings and plunging into the sea from on high, they hit the water in an awkward, loose-limbed crash that looks extremely hazardous.

But soon, up comes the white-crowned head, often with the tail of a wiggling fish protruding from its baggy, long-billed pouch. Pelicans feed around Alcatraz and occasionally roost on the island.

Snowy Egret

Among the most elegant of all birds, the egret has aigrettes (long, wispy white mating-season plumes) that were nearly its downfall. Eagerly sought for ladies' hats in the late 19th century, the decorative feathers were harvested via wholesale slaughter of the birds on their breeding grounds.

One of the environmental movement's success stories, the egret population has now recovered, and a snowy egret breeding colony can be found in the shrubs above the island's western cliffs.

Pigeon Guillemot

Another alcid (diving bird), these birds with red feet and white wing patches like to lay their eggs in Alcatraz's rocky crevices, just as they do at other sites on inaccessible islands or stretches of coastline. They bring a bit of ocean wildness to Alcatraz.

ALCATRAZ IS INDIANLAND

1969 – 1971

Aboriginal people of the San Francisco Bay Area, whom we now collectively dub "the Ohlone" (a Miwok term for "the West People"), likely did not paddle to Alcatraz often. It's parted from the mainland by a mile-wide gap of bay that's usually rough, frequently swept by swift tides, and always cold.

However, local lore suggests that this white-streaked lump of sandstone encircled by a wide moat of frigid water was sometimes used by the region's native people as a camp and resting spot during bay crossings, and as a one-stop shopping spot for seabird eggs during nesting season.

Alcatraz back then was probably barren of all but the most hardy vegetation, as well as liberally spattered—deeply coated, in all likelihood—with waterfowl droppings, or guano. The fact that the Gold Rush '49ers referred to Alcatraz as "Bird-dung Rock" (a sanitized version of what they actually called it) suggests its historic appearance. Back in the day, Alcatraz was likely a cold and stinky place.

Still, Bay Area native people could likely have gotten out there when they wanted to. Their watercraft, *balsas*—canoes made of long reed bundles lashed with twine made from native plant fibers—were buoyant, swift, and maneuverable (except in a strong head or beam breeze). Under certain circumstances, early European visitors discovered, those Indian balsas could be paddled faster than some of their own whaleboats could be rowed. (One wonders about the motives for such races.)

Given that they were present for at least fifteen centuries or so before Europeans appeared, it's likely that these tribal folk grasped a great deal about the workings of bay winds, waves, and tides. However, following Spanish incursion into and dominance of their traditional lands,

YOUNG ACTIVISTS, 1971; INTERNATIONAL VISITORS TO OCCUPIED ALCATRAZ, 1970; HAND-LETTERED SIGN OVER ADMINISTRATION WING ENTRY

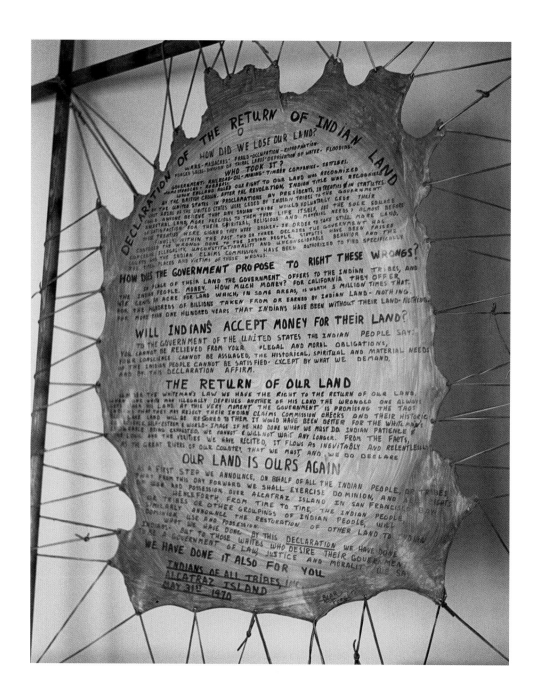

It would be fitting and symbolic that ships from all over the world entering the Golden Gate would first see Indian land, and thus be reminded of the true history of this nation.

— Richard Oakes (Mohawk), Occupation Spokesman

two centuries would pass before American Indians again made a big splash in this section of the bay. In 1964, not long after it was decommissioned as a prison island, Alcatraz was symbolically occupied by five Sioux Indians, who chartered a boat, landed on the island, claimed it under terms of a 1868 treaty, and then left. Then, on November 9, 1969, a 27-year-old Mohawk student activist from San Francisco State University named Richard Oakes dove over the rail of a Canadian sailing ship, the *Monte Cristo*, followed by six others. Swimming to Alcatraz to lay claim to the island in the name of all the US tribes, these young men effectively launched a protest that would last until June 1971, achieve world-wide renown, change the course of government policy toward Indians, and spark a lasting renewal of native pride and tribal power.

On that particular day, only a single young man was documented to have made landfall on the Rock, an Eskimo named Joe Bill, who happened to read the tidal currents correctly. By night-fall, all were back on the mainland. But they stubbornly made another try that night, and fourteen debarked from a commercial fishing boat onto Alcatraz. They left the next day after being threatened with arrest by government officials and federal marshals.

Then young Oakes—backed up by senior leaders of the protest, such as Adam Fortunate Eagle of the Bay Area United Indian Council—enlisted the aid of rambunctious waterfront denizens

1964 One year after it closes as a federal prison, the General Services Administration declares Alcatraz surplus government property. Ideas are floated for turning it into a Barbary Coast theme park, or other commercial development. Local citizens react with dismay.

1969 A National Park Service study concludes that the island would make a good national park. However, plans are derailed for two years by the Indian Occupation.

1970 Occupation begins to lose support as year goes on.

1971 Armed federal agents remove remainng occupiers from island.

1972 Golden Gate National Recreation Area is created, and Alcatraz is included under its protective umbrella.

AT LEFT: THE INDIANS OF ALL TRIBES RECORDED THEIR DEMANDS ON A PIECE OF TAUTLY STRETCHED HIDE.

In memory of Alcatraz, and as a symbol of my dedication to Indian causes, I have not cut my hair since. And as long as I live, I never will.

— Adam Fortunate Eagle (Red Lake Chippewa)

in the shoreline town of Sausalito, regulars at the infamous No Name Bar. On the night of November 20, ninety Indians from an array of tribes across the continent loaded camping supplies on three boats, weighed anchor, and disembarked on the Alcatraz dock. This time, they were there to stay.

And this time, word got out that their occupation of the island was no mere stunt. It was a protest against the hundreds of treaties that had been consistently violated in most of their particulars by the United States. It was a protest against the rip-off of tribal resources and the disastrous "relocation" policies begun in 1958, which were depopulating reservations (so they could be eliminated) and leaving Indians marooned in dead-end urban jobs.

Despite the seriousness of these points, the event did not lack humor. Adam Fortunate Eagle offered the Feds compensation for Alcatraz: twenty-four-dollars' worth of glass beads and red cloth—the same offer tendered by whites for the island of Manhattan three centuries earlier. And, it was noted, Alcatraz was

perfect for Indians, since it already had the hallmarks of reservation land: no health care, no modern plumbing, no schools, no industry or jobs, and very poor soil.

Richard Oakes, young, strong, and handsome, with a piercing gaze and a shock of wavy black hair, became the occupation's public face and spokesman. He did exceptionally well at it for six weeks. "Alcatraz is not an island, it's an idea," he said on one occasion. "The idea that you can recapture and be in control of your life, your destiny, and self-determine your future." This tiny island would be a symbol of the great lands once ruled by free and noble Indians.

Then, personal tragedy struck. One of the five Oakes children on the island with Richard and his wife Ann, 13-year-old Yvonne, died following a three-story fall down a stairwell in one of the occupied buildings. Soon after, Oakes left the island, saying, "You guys do what you can with it. I don't have the heart for it."

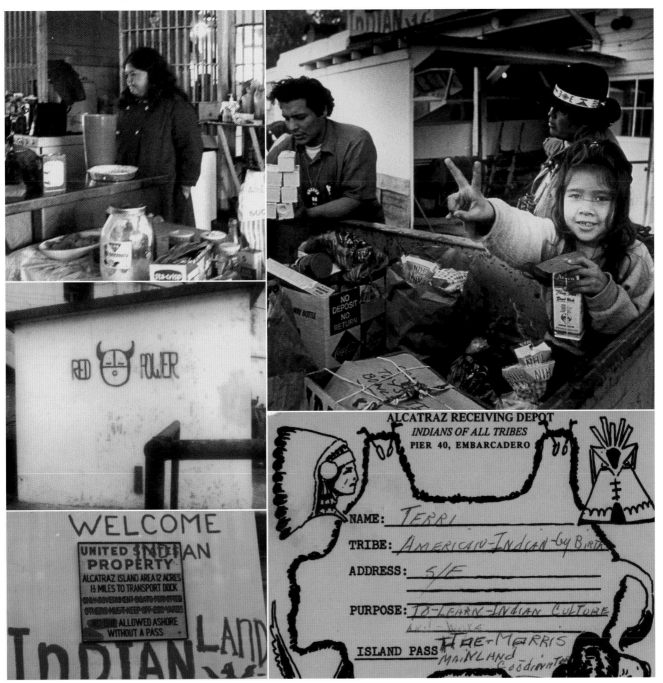

PRISON DINING HALL CONVERTED TO OCCUPIERS' USE; RICHARD OAKES (LEFT) HELPS UNLOAD SUPPLIES; OCCUPATION-ISSUED ISLAND PASS; GRAFFITI

From January 1970 onward, the occupation continued to make its points, drawing celebrity backing from the likes of Marlon Brando, Dick Gregory, Jonathan Winters, Jane Fonda, Anthony Quinn, and even the rock band Creedence Clearwater Revival. Initially well-organized and supported, the effort gradually fell apart due to infighting, vandalism and theft of island infrastructure, and infiltration by less idealistic elements of the popular culture.

Finally, a one-two-three punch brought the occupation down: the government towed away the island's water-supply barge; the warden's house, lighthouse keepers' houses, and other structures burned in a fire that the occupiers and the government accused one another of setting; and two tankers collided in the Golden Gate strait and spilled oil. Though lack of a lighthouse was not blamed for the collision, the public's patience and support for the occupation was exhausted. In June 1971, a force of federal marshals, FBI agents, and Coast Guard sailors ousted the last of the island's occupiers.

Oakes' short but flamboyant life was also near its end. Partially paralyzed in a bar brawl, in 1972 he was at a YMCA camp in Mendocino County, got into an argument over Indian boys riding horses, and was shot and killed by an armed and over-reactive camp manager. The killer was convicted of involuntary manslaughter, which enraged and galvanized tribes across the nation. Although a warrior's bow had been shattered, the arrow it launched continued to rise.

As Craig Glassner, long-time Alcatraz NPS ranger, says, "The Indian occupation may have been short, but it was the island's most significant episode. It ended the reservation termination program, and started the tribes down the path to self-determination."

In his book, *Alcatraz! Alcatraz!*, Adam Fortunate Eagle says, "Yet the most lasting result of Alcatraz may have been the growth of Indian pride throughout the country. News of the occupation swept through Indian communities; our continued resistance inspired wonder and pride."

AT RIGHT: DELEGATION FROM THE JAPANESE-AMERICAN ACTIVIST COMMUNITY TOURS THE CELLBLOCK, LED BY OCCUPIER STELLA LEACH (RIGHT), 1970.

The wind-blasted and guano-coated island was spared the gardener's trowel for thousands of years. It was not until people began living on it that gardens—indeed, any plants at all—could be seen on island.

What gardens offered: fields of color, fruits, and fragrance, reminders of more genteel locales. Outdoor gardening, a human activity, also provided fresh air, but a problem for the island-bound inmate population was that even a slight scent of freedom could prove terribly seductive.

And it did so for military-era prisoner Jesse Adams, serving life for slaying a fellow soldier in 1900. Adams' work detail was gardening, and he made use of his partial liberty to try to score quite a bit more. He had an accomplice nail him into a small crate, which was then delivered to a wharf, and then a warehouse, in San Francisco. Another accomplice is believed to have pried the crate open. It was a trick worthy of Houdini. But Adams was spotted and identified by a detective in Sacramento and dragged back to the hoosegow, never to be trusted with a hand-trowel again. Still, Adams is on the roster of folks who tried

to bestow more color and ambiance upon the Rock. That list ranges from an early lighthouse keeper and Freddie Reichel, Warden Johnston's secretary, to the children of prison guards, each of whom was awarded a tiny plot of thin soil to work as a hobby.

Soil, of course, was the quintessential ingredient. Originally, only modest amounts were imported for domestic horticultural purposes—in 1885, small garden plots framed officers' homes. The bulk of the imported soil and sod, brought onto the island by the barge-load, was used to create earthworks as protection for the fortified island's vertical brick walls.

Seeds of native flowering plants and grasses came along with the soil, of course. But gardeners were far from content with coyote brush. Once they had the soil base, they planted furiously: fuchsias, roses, and many other blooms; food plants ranging from figs to artichokes; and ornamentals such as Australian tea trees. Some horticultural experiments (mountain redwoods, *Sequoia gigantea*, for example) failed miserably. Others—opportunistic creepers like German ivy, mirror plant, and

IRIS IN BLOOM; CALIFORNIA POPPY; VICTORIAN-ERA CITADEL GARDEN; FEDERAL-PRISON-ERA INMATE GARDENER

> If we are all our own jailers and prisoners of our own traits, then I am grateful for my introduction to the spade and the trowel, the seed and the spray can. They have given me a lasting interest in creativity.
>
> — Elliot Michener, Inmate Gardener, AZ #578

Himalayan blackberry—succeeded beyond any-one's wildest nightmares. And so today, the Rock is home to at least 145 varieties of plants, an impressively lush riot of largely untended vegetation.

The harvest for humans was not just eye-catching beauty and bits and bites of fresh food, but also the peace that comes from kneeling on the earth and wrestling with the ancient issue of fertility.

At least one prisoner took to gardening and found in it an escape of another kind. Elliot Michener, a counterfeiter delivered to Alcatraz in 1941 to wear down a 30-year sentence, noted the dilapidated gardens and asked for and was given the chance to develop his green thumb. Michener built a tiny greenhouse near the old metal-detector building to nurture his efforts (only remnants of the structure's foundation remain), and a garden shed tucked between the end of West Road and the New Industries building (before the garden restoration project got underway, its frame and glass structure had almost disappeared under a wave of untended plant life). His legacy is found in the terraces on the west side of the cellhouse, where elegant yellow chasmanthe floribunda, Shasta daisies, red-hot pokers, and other plants flourish in the soil he deepened and enriched. Apparently, the work had a similar effect on him. After ten years beautifying the Rock, Michener was granted early release. It is reported that he went on to live a peaceful, productive, and law-abiding civilian life.

The National Park Service, Golden Gate National Parks Conservancy, and the Garden Conservancy have taken up the challenge of restoring selected historic gardens on the Rock, and have begun by landscaping the approach from the ferry dock to the old sally port. Eventually, the greenhouse and terraces on the west side may be restored to the elegant appearance they enjoyed in their heyday.

FOLLOW THE RANGER
A GARDEN TOUR

Agave

Once this desert specimen proved itself well-adapted to the island, it was widely planted to control erosion and improve the island's overall landscaping. The largest clusters are found south of the Parade Ground, along the aptly named Agave Trail.

Coyote Brush

These native bushes, drab most of the year, erupt in flat yellowish flowers (male) and long white plumes (female) each October. Big clusters, nesting sites for night herons, are found west of the lighthouse.

General MacArthur Rose

One of the most popular rose varieties of the early 1900s, this specimen's classic deep-red blooms can be seen on the north side of the warden's house ruin. It was named not for the hero of World War II, but for his father, Arthur MacArthur, who held the Pacific Command when Alcatraz was a military prison.

Fèlicitè et Pèrpetuè Rose

One of the antique varieties adorning the island, this rose, with its pale, elegant orbs, is most easily found in the terraces below the prison on the west side.

Athanasia

Hardy golden blooms of a South African import, *Athanasia parviflora*, can be found above the dock area, just south of the "bombproof barracks," Building 64.

Pride of Madeira

Possibly one of the most Alcatraz-appropriate plants, the Pride of Madeira does well all around the island, but is most prominent west of the cellhouse and south of the recreation yard walls, where in spring, its dramatic purple spikes decorate the landscape.

Fuchsia

Flamenco dancers of the botanical world, these downward-dangling, crimson-skirted flowers are also distributed across the island. 'Firecracker' and 'Mrs. Lovell Swisher' are present, and there's also 'Species Two,' or WH2, a variety more than a century old, for which we no longer have the common name. These are located at the north end of the dock, below the guard tower, and near the entrance to the sally port. The 'Rose of Castile' (shown here) has more delicate, purple pastel blooms—ballet dancers in tutus—than the first three. They are found on the north side of the sally port, where the road makes a switchback to the south.

Iceplant

A ground-hugging, drought-resistant plant appropriately known as "purple carpet," it flourishes on the slopes above the switchback where 'Rose of Castile' is found.

Torch Plant

These aloes are another successful import from the arid climes of South Africa. Their spiky blooms, ranging from orange to yellow, are found down on the lowest terraces on the west side of the cellhouse, just above the cliffs.

AT RIGHT: OXALIS FLOURISHES ALONG THE MAIN ROAD TO THE TOP OF THE ISLAND.

ALCATRAZ ISLAND TODAY

ALCATRAZ TODAY

Some national parks emphasize strong natural values; abundant wildlife and rare plants are embraced within such a preserve's circle of protection. Some offer displays of cultural and historic importance, artifacts that invoke major events in our human and national past.

Some parks seem to be primarily recreation areas, existing to present access to greenbelts and options for outdoor activity, investing visits with pleasure and charm.

Alcatraz achieves all three of these purposes quite handily. It would be hard to say which dimension dominates, as the dynamic shifts and evolves over the years. As of this writing, park managers are seeking to adjust the proportion of human access to wildlife habitat preservation on the island. Fine-tuning that balance is an ongoing process, one that reflects the NPS mission to—in the words of the 1916 National Park Service Organic Act—"conserve the scenery and the natural and historic objects and the wildlife therein and to provide for the enjoyment of the same in such manner and by such means as will leave them unimpaired for the enjoyment of future generations."

Hands-on Help

Once upon a time, people fought to keep away from Alcatraz; nowadays, folks fight to go. Well, perhaps "fight" is too strong a verb. But, during San Francisco's tourist season, it's not unusual to see long, winding lines of would-be visitors at the Alcatraz-bound ferry terminal. It's pretty clear that desire is high, but opportunity is limited.

Yet, there's more than one way to become a temporary denizen of "America's Devil's Island." Join that throng of eager visitors… or, better yet, guide them. Among opportunities that the National Park Service provides here (and in its other units as well) are full and part-time internships and volunteer opportunities. On Alcatraz, tasks can include guiding public tours, offering interpretation of the historic and natural sites, assisting park staff in research, complementing the park's office and clerical staff, and gardening. For more information, go to the Golden Gate National Recreation Area Web page and click on "volunteer," or phone (415) 561-4755.

The Golden Gate National Parks Conservancy, the nonprofit support group that helps keep this collection of parks vibrant and functioning, also numbers volunteer work parties on Alcatraz among its activities. One ongoing project is restoring the island's exotic and native plant gardens. For more information, take a look at the Conservancy's website.

Collaborating with the NPS and the Parks Conservancy is a national organization, the Garden Conservancy, which helps preserve gardens under its Preservation Projects Program. The gardens on Alcatraz were selected for inclusion in this program based on their horticultural, aesthetic, historical, and cultural significance.

Volunteering is an excellent route to in-depth experiences on this most intriguing of islands. And you'll have the satisfaction of knowing that you've not only enhanced your experience, you've contributed to enhancing the park itself, as well as the experience of others.

To paraphrase American folk singer Woody Guthrie, these parks were made for you and me.

ON THE WEB

National Park Service/Golden Gate National Recreation Area
www.nps.gov/goga

Golden Gate National Parks Conservancy
www.parksconservancy.org

Garden Conservancy
www.gardenconservancy.org

Museum Collections at the Rock
www.cr.nps.gov/museum/exhibits/alca/overview.html

1973 Alcatraz opens to the public; park officials believe that interest in the island will wane after a few years.

1984 Not only does Alcatraz remain open as a public park, its popularity steadily soars. Rangers dispense with the traditional two-hour guided tour, and visitors are able to stay on the island as long as there's a ferry running.

2001 A new master plan for the island park is finalized. A $5 million prison stabilization program begins, to ensure seismic safety and keep the island's main attraction, the prison building, accessible.

2004 The National Park Service, Golden Gate National Parks Conservancy, and Garden Conservancy take on the job of restoring selected Alcatraz gardens, legacies of both the military and federal prison years.

2006 The Alcatraz visitor experience is enhanced with new exhibits, audio tours, and bookstore space.

Library of Congress Control Number: 2005937478
ISBN 978-1-883869-08-3

PARKS FOR ALL
FOREVER

The Golden Gate National Parks Conservancy is a nonprofit membership
organization created to help preserve the Golden Gate National Parks,
enhance the experiences of park visitors, and build a community dedicated
to conserving the parks for the future. For more information, please phone
(415) 4R-PARKS or visit *www.parksconservancy.org*.

Historical Consultant: John A. Martini
Editor and Project Manager: Susan Tasaki
Cover and Interior Design: Bill Reuter/Reuter Design

Printed on FSC-certified paper in Hong Kong

"Flooding the Bay" map, p. 11: US Geological Society
Alcatraz map, p. 12: Haisam Hussein

All artifacts included in this book are from the National Park Service Museum
Collection, Golden Gate National Recreation Area; see more online at
www.cr.nps.gov/museum/exhibits/alca/overview.html.

PHOTO CREDITS
Photographs included in this book come from a variety of sources and are
either copyrighted or may have other use restrictions. Please contact the
individual or archive cited with use-related questions.

COVER
Mike Long/Alamy (top); John Louie (bottom)

CONTEMPORARY
Roy Eisenhardt: pp. ii–iii, v, vi, viii–ix, x, 2 (gulls, garden shed), 7 (doorway),
8, 9, 10, 24 (guard tower, warden's house, San Francisco views, roosting
seabirds, nesting gulls), 39 (cormorants), 40 (Brandt's cormorant, black-
crowned night heron, snowy egret), 53 (iris, California poppy), 54, 56
(agave, General MacArthur rose, Pride of Madeira, fuchsia, iceplant, torch
plant), 57, 58–59

Will Elder: p. 39 (brown pelican), 41 (brown pelican detail)

Golden Gate National Parks Conservancy Collection: pp. 40 (common
murre, Canada goose, black oystercatcher, Western grebe, pigeon guillemot),
56 (athanasia), 60

Ryan Jones: pp. 40 (Anna's hummingbird), 56 (coyote brush)

Robert Lieber: pp. 24 (sally port garden, prison entry, rec yard door),
56 (Fèlicitè et Pèrpetuè rose)

Mindy Manville: p. 24 (wild garden)

James A. Martin: Inside front cover/title page, pp. 7 (lower right, lighthouse),
25, 36

John Martini: pp. 26–27

National Park Service: pp. 2 (hospital cell; view toward Bay Bridge), 4

Jim Robertson/animalsinthewild.com: p. 38

Brenda Tharp: pp. 7 (gull nest and eggs), 24 (nesting shorebirds), 39 (gull
and chick)

HISTORICAL
All historical photographs are from the Golden Gate National Recreation
Area/Park Archives and Records Center unless otherwise noted below.
Further information can be found online at
www.cr.nps.gov/museum/exhibits/alca/overview.html.

Bancroft Library, University of California, Berkeley: pp. 14–15 (BANC PIC
1960.010, ser. 2:0508), 23 (BANC 1971.055, ser. 1, v. 2, no. 638)

Rod Crossley Collection: p. 20 (top left, soldier walking up road)

Michael Esslinger Collection: p. 16 (top right, soldiers at dock area)

Ilka Hartmann: pp. 44, 45 (top, young activists), 46, 50

San Francisco Chronicle: p. 49 (top right, Richard Oakes unloading truck)

San Francisco Public Library: p. 20 (upper right, pre-1909 lighthouse/
AAC-9317), 31 ("Broadway"/AAC-9384)

Joseph H. Simpson: p. 53 (lower left, inmate gardener)

Isao Tanaka/National Japanese-American Historical Society: pp. 45 (lower
right, visitors to island), 51

Michelle Vignes: p. 49 (top left, dining hall/detail)

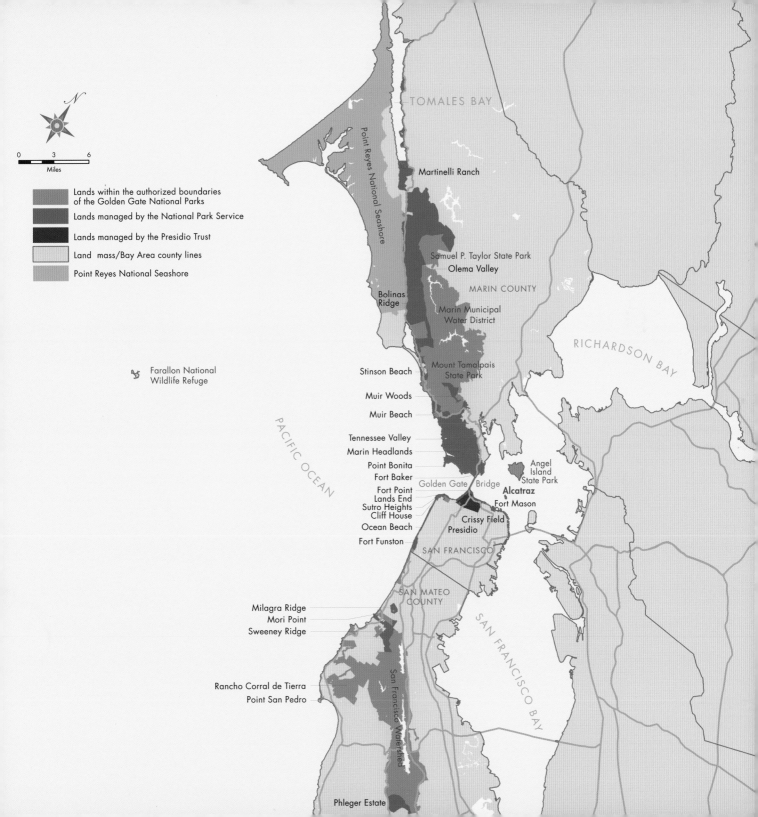

N

| | 0 | 3 | 6 |
Miles

Lands within the authorized boundaries
of the Golden Gate National Parks

Lands managed by the National Park Service

Lands managed by the Presidio Trust

Land mass/Bay Area county lines

Point Reyes National Seashore

TOMALES BAY

Martinelli Ranch

Point Reyes National Seashore

Samuel P. Taylor State Park
Olema Valley

MARIN COUNTY

Bolinas
Ridge

Marin Municipal
Water District

RICHARDSON BAY

Mount Tamalpais
State Park

Stinson Beach

Farallon National
Wildlife Refuge

Muir Woods

Muir Beach

PACIFIC OCEAN

Tennessee Valley

Marin Headlands

Point Bonita

Angel
Island
State Park

Fort Baker

Golden Gate Bridge   Alcatraz

Fort Point   Fort Mason
Lands End
Sutro Heights
Cliff House   Crissy Field
Ocean Beach   Presidio

Fort Funston

SAN FRANCISCO

SAN MATEO
COUNTY

Milagra Ridge
Mori Point

SAN FRANCISCO BAY

Sweeney Ridge

Rancho Corral de Tierra

San Francisco Watershed

Point San Pedro

Phleger Estate